THE RAPE OF LUCRECE

WILLIAM SHAKESPEARE

THE RAPE OF
LUCRECE

Illustrated by

J. YUNGE-BATEMAN

WINCHESTER PUBLICATIONS LIMITED
LONDON

Published in mcmxlviii by
Winchester Publications Limited
16 Maddox Street, London, W.1

The text is that of "The Pictorial
Edition of the Works of Shakspere"
edited by Charles Knight and
published by Charles Knight and
Co., London, in 1841.

MADE AND PRINTED IN GREAT BRITAIN BY L. T. A. ROBINSON, LTD., LONDON, S.W.9

To the Right Honourable
HENRY WRIOTHESLY
EARL OF SOUTHAMPTON AND BARON OF TITCHFIELD

THE LOVE I dedicate to your Lordship is without end; whereof this pamphlet, without beginning, is but a superfluous moiety. The warrant I have of your honourable disposition, not the worth of my untutored lines, makes it assured of acceptance. What I have done is yours, what I have to do is yours; being part in all I have, devoted yours. Were my worth greater my duty would show greater: meantime, as it is, it is bound to your Lordship, to whom I wish long life, still lengthened with all happiness.

Your Lordship's in all duty,

WILLIAM SHAKESPEARE

THE ARGUMENT

LUCIUS TARQUINIUS (*for his excessive pride surnamed Superbus*), *after he had caused his own father-in-law, Servius Tullius, to be cruelly murdered, and, contrary to the Roman laws and customs, not requiring or staying for the people's suffrages, had possessed himself of the kingdom, went, accompanied with his sons and other noblemen of Rome, to besiege Ardea. During which siege the principal men of the army meeting one evening at the tent of Sextus Tarquinius, the king's son, in their discourses after supper, every one commended the virtues of his own wife ; among whom, Collatinus extolled the incomparable chastity of his wife Lucretia. In that pleasant humour they all posted to Rome ; and intending, by their secret and sudden arrival, to make trial of that which every one had before avouched, only Collatinus finds his wife (though it were late in the night) spinning amongst her maids ; the other ladies were all found dancing and revelling, or in several disports. Whereupon the noblemen yielded Collatinus the victory, and his wife the fame. At that time Sextus Tarquinius, being inflamed with Lucrece' beauty, yet smothering his passions for the present, departed with the rest back to the camp ; from whence he shortly after privily withdrew himself, and was (according to his estate) royally entertained and lodged by Lucrece at Collatium. The same night he treacherously stealeth into her chamber, violently ravished her, and early in the morning speedeth away. Lucrece, in this lamentable plight, hastily despatcheth messengers, one to Rome for her father, another to the camp for Collatine. They came, the one accompanied with Junius Brutus, the other with Publius Valerius ; and, finding Lucrece attired in mourning habit, demanded the cause of her sorrow. She, first taking an oath of them for her revenge, revealed the actor, and whole manner of his dealing, and withal suddenly stabbed herself. Which done, with one consent they all vowed to root out the whole hated family of the Tarquins ; and, bearing the dead body to Rome, Brutus acquainted the people with the doer and manner of the vile deed, with a bitter invective against the tyranny of the king : wherewith the people were so moved, that with one consent and a general acclamation the Tarquins were all exiled, and the state government changed from kings to consuls.*

THE RAPE OF LUCRECE

From the besieged Ardea all in post,
Borne by the trustless wings of false desire,
Lust-breathed Tarquin leaves the Roman host,
And to Collatium bears the lightless fire
Which, in pale embers hid, lurks to aspire,
    And girdle with embracing flames the waist
    Of Collatine's fair love, Lucrece the chaste.

Haply that name of chaste unhapp'ly set
This bateless edge on his keen appetite ;
When Collatine unwisely did not let
To praise the clear unmatched red and white
Which triumph'd in that sky of his delight,
    Where mortal stars, as bright as heaven's beauties,
    With pure aspects did him peculiar duties.

For he the night before, in Tarquin's tent,
Unlock'd the treasure of his happy state ;
What priceless wealth the heavens had him lent
In the possession of his beauteous mate ;
Reckoning his fortune at such high-proud rate,
    That kings might be espoused to more fame,
    But king nor peer to such a peerless dame.

O happiness enjoy'd but of a few !
And, if possess'd, as soon decay'd and done
As is the morning's silver-melting dew
Against the golden splendour of the sun !
An expir'd date, cancell'd ere well begun :
   Honour and beauty, in the owner's arms,
   Are weakly fortress'd from a world of harms.

Beauty itself doth of itself persuade
The eyes of men without an orator ;
What needeth then apologies be made
To set forth that which is so singular ?
Or why is Collatine the publisher
   Of that rich jewel he should keep unknown
   From thievish ears, because it is his own ?

Perchance his boast of Lucrece' sovereignty
Suggested this proud issue of a king ;
For by our ears our hearts oft tainted be :
Perchance that envy of so rich a thing,
Braving compare, disdainfully did sting
   His high-pitch'd thoughts, that meaner men should vaunt
   That golden hap which their superiors want.

But some untimely thought did instigate
His all-too-timeless speed, if none of those :
His honour, his affairs, his friends, his state,
Neglected all, with swift intent he goes
To quench the coal which in his liver glows.
   O rash false heat, wrapp'd in repentant cold,
   Thy hasty spring still blasts, and ne'er grows old !

When at Collatium this false lord arriv'd,
Well was he welcom'd by the Roman dame,
Within whose face beauty and virtue striv'd
Which of them both should underprop her fame :
When virtue bragg'd, beauty would blush for shame ;
  When beauty boasted blushes, in despite
  Virtue would stain that or with silver white.

But beauty, in that white intituled,
From Venus' doves doth challenge that fair field :
Then virtue claims from beauty beauty's red,
Which virtue gave the golden age, to gild
Their silver cheeks, and call'd it then their shield ;
  Teaching them thus to use it in the fight,—
  When shame assail'd, the red should fence the white.

This heraldry in Lucrece' face was seen,
Argued by beauty's red, and virtue's white :
Of either's colour was the other queen,
Proving from world's minority their right :
Yet their ambition makes them still to fight ;
  The sovereignty of either being so great,
  That oft they interchange each other's seat.

This silent war of lilies and of roses
Which Tarquin view'd in her fair face's field,
In their pure ranks his traitor eye encloses ;
Where, lest between them both it should be kill'd,
The coward captive vanquished doth yield
  To those two armies that would let him go,
  Rather than triumph in so false a foe.

Now thinks he that her husband's shallow tongue
(The niggard prodigal that prais'd her so)
In that high task hath done her beauty wrong,
Which far exceeds his barren skill to show :
Therefore that praise which Collatine doth owe,
   Enchanted Tarquin answers with surmise,
   In silent wonder of still-gazing eyes.

This earthly saint, adored by this devil,
Little suspecteth the false worshipper ;
For unstain'd thoughts do seldom dream on evil ;
Birds never lim'd no secret bushes fear :
So guiltless she securely gives good cheer
   And reverend welcome to her princely guest,
   Whose inward ill no outward harm express'd :

For that he colour'd with his high estate,
Hiding base sin in plaits of majesty ;
That nothing in him seem'd inordinate,
Save sometime too much wonder of his eye,
Which, having all, all could not satisfy ;
   But, poorly rich, so wanteth in his store
   That cloy'd with much he pineth still for more.

But she, that never cop'd with stranger eyes,
Could pick no meaning from their parling looks,
Nor read the subtle-shining secrecies
Writ in the glassy margents of such books ;
She touch'd no unknown baits, nor fear'd no hooks ;
   Nor could she moralize his wanton sight,
   More than his eyes were open'd to the light.

*What priceless wealth the heavens had him lent
In the possession of his beauteous mate*

He stories to her ears her husband's fame,
Won in the fields of fruitful Italy ;
And decks with praises Collatine's high name,
Made glorious by his manly chivalry,
With bruised arms and wreaths of victory ;
    Her joy with heav'd-up hand she doth express,
    And, wordless, so greets heaven for his success.

Far from the purpose of his coming thither,
He makes excuses for his being there.
No cloudy show of stormy blustering weather
Doth yet in his fair welkin once appear ;
Till sable Night, mother of Dread and Fear,
    Upon the world dim darkness doth display,
    And in her vaulty prison stows the day.

For then is Tarquin brought unto his bed,
Intending weariness with heavy spright ;
For, after supper, long he questioned
With modest Lucrece, and wore out the night :
Now leaden slumber with life's strength doth fight ;
    And every one to rest himself betakes,
    Save thieves, and cares, and troubled minds, that wakes.

As one of which doth Tarquin lie revolving
The sundry dangers of his will's obtaining ;
Yet ever to obtain his will resolving,
Though weak-built hopes persuade him to abstaining ;
Despair to gain doth traffic oft for gaining ;
    And when great treasure is the meed propos'd,
    Though death be adjunct, there's no death suppos'd.

Those that much covet are with gain so fond,
That what they have not, that which they possess
They scatter and unloose it from their bond,
And so, by hoping more, they have but less;
Or, gaining more, the profit of excess
    Is but to surfeit, and such griefs sustain,
    That they prove bankrupt in this poor-rich gain.

The aim of all is but to nurse the life
With honour, wealth, and ease, in waning age;
And in this aim there is such thwarting strife,
That one for all, or all for one we gage;
As life for honour in fell battles' rage;
    Honour for wealth; and oft that wealth doth cost
    The death of all, and all together lost.

So that in vent'ring ill we leave to be
The things we are, for that which we expect;
And this ambitious foul infirmity,
In having much, torments us with defect
Of that we have: so then we do neglect
    The thing we have, and, all for want of wit,
    Make something nothing, by augmenting it.

Such hazard now must doting Tarquin make,
Pawning his honour to obtain his lust;
And for himself himself he must forsake:
Then where is truth if there be no self-trust?
When shall he think to find a stranger just,
    When he himself himself confounds, betrays
    To slanderous tongues, and wretched hateful days?

When at the Collatium this false lord arriv'd,
Well was he welcom'd by the Roman dame

Now stole upon the time the dead of night,
When heavy sleep had clos'd up mortal eyes ;
No comfortable star did lend his light,
No noise but owls' and wolves' death-boding cries ;
Now serves the season that they may surprise
    The silly lambs ; pure thoughts are dead and still,
    While lust and murder wake to stain and kill.

And now this lustful lord leap'd from his bed,
Throwing his mantle rudely o'er his arm ;
Is madly toss'd between desire and dread ;
Th' one sweetly flatters, th' other feareth harm ;
But honest Fear, bewitch'd with lust's foul charm,
    Doth too too oft betake him to retire,
    Beaten away by brain-sick rude Desire.

His falchion on a flint he softly smiteth,
That from the cold stone sparks of fire do fly,
Whereat a waxen torch forthwith he lighteth,
Which must be lode-star to his lustful eye ;
And to the flame thus speaks advisedly :
    " As from this cold flint I enforc'd this fire,
    So Lucrece must I force to my desire."

Here pale with fear he doth premeditate
The dangers of his loathsome enterprise,
And in his inward mind he doth debate
What following sorrow may on this arise ;
Then looking scornfully, he doth despise
    His naked armour of still-slaughter'd lust,
    And justly thus controls his thoughts unjust :

" Fair torch, burn out thy light, and lend it not
To darken her whose light excelleth thine !
And die unhallow'd thoughts, before you blot
With your uncleanness that which is divine !
Offer pure incense to so pure a shrine :
  Let fair humanity abhor the deed
  That spots and stains love's modest snow-white weed.

" O shame to knighthood and to shining arms !
O foul dishonour to my household's grave !
O impious act, including all foul harms !
A martial man to be soft fancy's slave ;
True valour still a true respect should have ;
  Then my digression is so vile, so base,
  That it will live engraven in my face.

" Yea, though I die, the scandal will survive,
And be an eyesore in my golden coat ;
Some loathsome dash the herald will contrive,
To cipher me how fondly I did dote ;
That my posterity, sham'd with the note,
  Shall curse my bones, and hold it for no sin
  To wish that I their father had not been.

" What win I if I gain the thing I seek ?
A dream, a breath, a froth of fleeting joy :
Who buys a minute's mirth to wail a week ?
Or sells eternity to get a toy ?
For one sweet grape who will the vine destroy ?
  Or what fond beggar, but to touch the crown,
  Would with the sceptre straight be strucken down ?

" If Collatinus dream of my intent
Will he not wake, and in a desperate rage
Post hither, this vile purpose to prevent ?
This siege that hath engirt his marriage,
This blur to youth, this sorrow to the sage,
    This dying virtue, this surviving shame,
    Whose crime will bear an ever-during blame ?

" O what excuse can my invention make,
When thou shalt charge me with so black a deed ?
Will not my tongue be mute, my frail joints shake ?
Mine eyes forego their light, my false heart bleed ?
The guilt being great the fear doth still exceed ;
    And extreme fear can neither fight nor fly,
    But, coward-like, with trembling terror die.

" Had Collatinus kill'd my son or sire,
Or lain in ambush to betray my life,
Or were he not my dear friend, this desire
Might have excuse to work upon his wife ;
As in revenge or quittal of such strife :
    But as he is my kinsman, my dear friend,
    The shame and fault finds no excuse nor end.

" Shameful it is ; — ay, if the fact be known :
Hateful it is ; — there is no hate in loving :
I'll beg her love ; — but she is not her own ;
The worst is but denial, and reproving :
My will is strong, past reason's weak removing.
    Who fears a sentence or an old man's saw
    Shall by a painted cloth be kept in awe."

Thus, graceless, holds he disputation
'Tween frozen conscience and hot-burning will,
And with good thoughts makes dispensation,
Urging the worser sense for vantage still;
Which in a moment doth confound and kill
 All pure effects, and doth so far proceed,
 That what is vile shows like a virtuous deed.

Quoth he, "She took me kindly by the hand,
And gaz'd for tidings in my eager eyes,
Fearing some hard news from the warlike band
Where her beloved Collatinus lies.
O how her fear did make her colour rise!
 First red as roses that on lawn we lay,
 Then white as lawn, the roses took away.

" And how her hand, in my hand being lock'd,
Forc'd it to tremble with her loyal fear;
Which struck her sad, and then it faster rock'd,
Until her husband's welfare she did hear;
Whereat she smiled with so sweet a cheer,
 That had Narcissus seen her as she stood,
 Self-love had never drown'd him in the flood.

" Why hunt I then for colour or excuses?
All orators are dumb when beauty pleadeth;
Poor wretches have remorse in poor abuses;
Love thrives not in the heart that shadows dreadeth:
Affection is my captain, and he leadeth;
 And when his gaudy banner is display'd,
 The coward fights, and will not be dismay'd.

'*If Collatinus dream of my intent*
Will he not wake . . . . ?'

" Then, childish fear, avaunt ! debating, die !
Respect and reason wait on wrinkled age !
My heart shall never countermand mine eye :
Sad pause and deep regard beseem the sage ;
My part is youth, and beats these from the stage :
    Desire my pilot is, beauty my prize ;
    Then who fears sinking where such treasure lies ? "

As corn o'ergrown by weeds, so heedful fear
Is almost chok'd by unresisted lust.
Away he steals with open listening ear,
Full of foul hope, and full of fond mistrust ;
Both which, as servitors to the unjust,
    So cross him with their opposite persuasion,
    That now he vows a league, and now invasion.

Within his thought her heavenly image sits,
And in the selfsame seat sits Collatine :
That eye which looks on her confounds his wits ;
That eye which him beholds, as more divine,
Unto a view so false will not incline ;
    But with a pure appeal seeks to the heart,
    Which once corrupted takes the worser part ;

And therein heartens up his servile powers,
Who, flatter'd by their leader's jocund show,
Stuff up his lust, as minutes fill up hours ;
And as their captain, so their pride doth grow,
Paying more slavish tribute than they owe.
    By reprobate desire thus madly led,
    The Roman lord marcheth to Lucrece' bed.

The locks between her chamber and his will,
Each one by him enforc'd, retires his ward ;
But as they open they all rate his ill,
Which drives the creeping thief to some regard ;
The threshold grates the door to have him heard ;
  Night-wand'ring weasels shriek to see him there ;
  They fright him, yet he still pursues his fear.

As each unwilling portal yields him way,
Through little vents and crannies of the place
The wind wars with his torch, to make him stay,
And blows the smoke of it into his face,
Extinguishing his conduct in this case ;
  But his hot heart, which fond desire doth scorch,
  Puffs forth another wind that fires the torch :

And being lighted, by the light he spies
Lucretia's glove, wherein her needle sticks ;
He takes it from the rushes where it lies,
And griping it, the neeld his finger pricks :
As who should say, this glove to wanton tricks
  Is not inur'd ; return again in haste ;
  Thou seest our mistress' ornaments are chaste.

But all these poor forbiddings could not stay him ;
He in the worst sense construes their denial :
The doors, the wind, the glove that did delay him,
He takes for accidental things of trial ;
Or as those bars which stop the hourly dial,
  Who with a lingering stay his course doth let,
  Till every minute pays the hour his debt

Within his thought her heavenly image sits,
And in the selfsame seat sits Collatine

"So, so," quoth he, "these lets attend the time,
Like little frosts that sometime threat the spring,
To add a more rejoicing to the prime,
To give the sneaped birds more cause to sing.
Pain pays the income of each precious thing ;
    Huge rocks, high winds, strong pirates, shelves and sands,
    The merchant fears, ere rich at home he lands."

Now is he come unto the chamber door
That shuts him from the heaven of his thought,
Which with a yielding latch, and with no more,
Hath barr'd him from the blessed thing he sought.
So from himself impiety hath wrought,
    That for his prey to pray he doth begin,
    As if the heaven should countenance his sin.

But in the midst of his unfruitful prayer,
Having solicited the eternal power,
That his foul thoughts might compass his fair fair,
And they would stand auspicious to the hour,
Even there he starts : — quoth he, " I must deflower ;
    The powers to whom I pray abhor this fact,
    How can they then assist me in the act ?

" Then Love and Fortune be my gods, my guide !
My will is back'd with resolution :
Thoughts are but dreams till their effects be tried,
The blackest sin is clear'd with absolution ;
Against love's fire fear's frost hath dissolution.
    The eye of heaven is out, and misty night
    Covers the shame that follows sweet delight."

This said, his guilty hand pluck'd up the latch,
And with his knee the door he opens wide :
The dove sleeps fast that this night-owl will catch ;
Thus treason works ere traitors be espied.
Who sees the lurking serpent steps aside ;
    But she, sound sleeping, fearing no such thing,
    Lies at the mercy of his mortal sting.

Into the chamber wickedly he stalks,
And gazeth on her yet unstained bed.
The curtains being close, about he walks,
Rolling his greedy eyeballs in his head :
By their high treason is his heart misled ;
    Which gives the watchword to his hand full soon,
    To draw the cloud that hides the silver moon.

Look, as the fair and fiery-pointed sun,
Rushing from forth a cloud, bereaves our sight ;
Even so, the curtain drawn, his eyes begun
To wink, being blinded with a greater light :
Whether it is that she reflects so bright,
    That dazzleth them, or else some shame supposed ;
    But blind they are, and keep themselves enclosed.

O, had they in that darksome prison died,
Then had they seen the period of their ill !
Then Collatine again by Lucrece' side
In his clear bed might have reposed still :
But they must ope, this blessed league to kill ;
    And holy-thoughted Lucrece to their sight
    Must sell her joy, her life, her world's delight.

Her lily hand her rosy cheek lies under,
Cozening the pillow of a lawful kiss ;
Who therefore angry, seems to part in sunder,
Swelling on either side to want his bliss ;
Between whose hills her head entombed is :
    Where, like a virtuous monument, she lies,
    To be admir'd of lewd unhallow'd eyes.

Without the bed her other fair hand was,
On the green coverlet ; whose perfect white
Show'd like an April daisy on the grass,
With pearly sweat, resembling dew of night.
Her eyes, like marigolds, had sheath'd their light,
    And canopied in darkness sweetly lay,
    Till they might open to adorn the day.

Her hair, like golden threads, play'd with her breath ;
O modest wantons ! wanton modesty !
Showing life's triumph in the map of death,
And death's dim look in life's mortality :
Each in her sleep themselves so beautify,
    As if between them twain there were no strife,
    But that life liv'd in death, and death in life.

Her breasts, like ivory globes circled with blue,
A pair of maiden worlds unconquered,
Save of their lord no bearing yoke they knew,
And him by oath they truly honoured.
These worlds in Tarquin new ambition bred :
    Who, like a foul usurper, went about
    From this fair throne to heave the owner out.

What could he see but mightily he noted?
What did he note but strongly he desir'd?
What he beheld on that he firmly doted,
And in his will his wilful eye he tir'd.
With more than admiration he admir'd
    Her azure veins, her alabaster skin,
    Her coral lips, her snow-white dimpled chin.

As the grim lion fawneth o'er his prey,
Sharp hunger by the conquest satisfied,
So o'er this sleeping soul doth Tarquin stay,
His rage of lust by gazing qualified ;
Slack'd, not suppress'd ; for standing by her side,
    His eye, which late this mutiny restrains,
    Unto a greater uproar tempts his veins :

And they, like straggling slaves for pillage fighting,
Obdurate vassals, fell exploits effecting,
In bloody death and ravishment delighting,
Nor children's tears, nor mother's groans respecting,
Swell in their pride, the onset still expecting :
    Anon his beating heart, alarum striking,
    Gives the hot charge, and bids them do their liking.

His drumming heart cheers up his burning eye,
His eye commends the leading to his hand ;
His hand, as proud of such a dignity,
Smoking with pride, march'd on to make his stand
On her bare breast, the heart of all her land ;
    Whose ranks of blue veins, as his hand did scale,
    Left their round turrets destitute and pale.

32

Where, like a virtuous monument, she lies,
To be admir'd of lewd unhallow'd eyes

They, mustering to the quiet cabinet
Where their dear governess and lady lies,
Do tell her she is dreadfully beset,
And fright her with confusion of their cries :
She, much amaz'd, breaks ope her lock'd-up eyes,
  Who, peeping forth this tumult to behold,
  Are by his flaming torch dimm'd and controll'd.

Imagine her as one in dead of night
From forth dull sleep by dreadful fancy waking,
That thinks she hath beheld some ghastly sprite,
Whose grim aspect sets every joint a shaking ;
What terror 't is ! but she, in worser taking,
  From sleep disturbed, heedfully doth view
  The sight which makes supposed terror true.

Wrapp'd and confounded in a thousand fears,
Like to a new-kill'd bird she trembling lies ;
She dares not look ; yet, winking, there appears
Quick-shifting antics, ugly in her eyes :
Such shadows are the weak brain's forgeries :
  Who, angry that the eyes fly from their lights,
  In darkness daunts them with more dreadful sights.

His hand, that yet remains upon her breast,
(Rude ram, to batter such an ivory wall !)
May feel her heart, poor citizen, distress'd,
Wounding itself to death, rise up and fall,
Beating her bulk, that his hand shakes withal.
  This moves in him more rage, and lesser pity,
  To make the breach, and enter this sweet city.

First, like a trumpet, doth his tongue begin
To sound a parley to his heartless foe,
Who o'er the white sheet peers her whiter chin,
The reason of this rash alarm to know,
Which he by dumb demeanour seeks to show;
  But she with vehement prayers urgeth still
  Under what colour he commits this ill.

Thus he replies : " The colour in thy face
(That even for anger makes the lily pale,
And the red rose blush at her own disgrace)
Shall plead for me, and tell my loving tale :
Under that colour am I come to scale
  Thy never-conquer'd fort ; the fault is thine,
  For those thine eyes betray thee unto mine.

" Thus I forestall thee, if thou mean to chide :
Thy beauty hath ensnar'd thee to this night,
Where thou with patience must my will abide,
My will that marks thee for my earth's delight,
Which I to conquer sought with all my might ;
  But as reproof and reason beat it dead,
  By thy bright beauty was it newly bred.

" I see what crosses my attempt will bring ;
I know what thorns the growing rose defends ;
I think the honey guarded with a sting :
All this, beforehand, counsel comprehends :
But will is deaf, and hears no heedful friends ;
  Only he hath an eye to gaze on beauty,
  And dotes on what he looks, 'gainst law or duty.

'*Wilt thou be glass, wherein it shall discern*
Authority for sin, warrant for blame?'

" I have debated, even in my soul,
What wrong, what shame, what sorrow I shall breed ;
But nothing can Affection's course control,
Or stop the headlong fury of his speed.
I know repentant tears ensue the deed,
    Reproach, disdain, and deadly enmity ;
    Yet strive I to embrace mine infamy."

This said, he shakes aloft his Roman blade,
Which, like a falcon towering in the skies,
Coucheth the fowl below with his wing's shade,
Whose crooked beak threats if he mount he dies :
So under his insulting falchion lies
    Harmless Lucretia, marking what he tells
    With trembling fear, as fowl hear falcon's bells.

" Lucrece," quoth he, " this night I must enjoy thee :
If thou deny, then force must work my way,
For in thy bed I purpose to destroy thee ;
That done, some worthless slave of thine I'll slay,
To kill thine honour with thy life's decay ;
    And in thy dead arms do I mean to place him,
    Swearing I slew him, seeing thee embrace him.

" So thy surviving husband shall remain
The scornful mark of every open eye ;
Thy kinsmen hang their heads at this disdain,
Thy issue blurr'd with nameless bastardy :
And thou, the author of their obloquy,
    Shalt have thy trespass cited up in rhymes,
    And sung by children in succeeding times.

" But if thou yield I rest thy secret friend :
The fault unknown is as a thought unacted ;
A little harm, done to a great good end,
For lawful policy remains enacted.
The poisonous simple sometimes is compacted
  In a pure compound ; being so applied
  His venom in effect is purified.

" Then for thy husband and thy children's sake,
Tender my suit : bequeath not to their lot
The shame that from them no device can take,
The blemish that will never be forgot ;
Worse than a slavish wipe, or birth-hour's blot :
  For marks descried in men's nativity
  Are nature's faults, not their own infamy."

Here with a cockatrice' dead-killing eye
He rouseth up himself, and makes a pause ;
While she, the picture of pure piety,
Like a white hind under the grype's sharp claws,
Pleads in a wilderness, where are no laws,
  To the rough beast that knows no gentle right,
  Nor aught obeys but his foul appetite :

But when a black-fac'd cloud the world doth threat,
In his dim mist the aspiring mountains hiding,
From earth's dark womb some gentle gust doth get,
Which blows these pitchy vapours from their biding,
Hindering their present fall by this dividing ;
  So his unhallow'd haste her words delays,
  And moody Pluto winks while Orpheus plays.

Yet, foul night-waking cat, he doth but dally,
While in his holdfast foot the weak mouse panteth ;
Her sad behaviour feeds his vulture folly,
A swallowing gulf that even in plenty wanteth :
His ear her prayers admits, but his heart granteth
  No penetrable entrance to her plaining :
  Tears harden lust, though marble wear with raining.

Her pity-pleading eyes are sadly fix'd
In the remorseless wrinkles of his face ;
Her modest eloquence with sighs is mix'd,
Which to her oratory adds more grace.
She puts the period often from his place,
  And 'midst the sentence so her accent breaks,
  That twice she doth begin ere once she speaks.

She conjures him by high almighty Jove,
By knighthood, gentry, and sweet friendship's oath,
By her untimely tears, her husband's love,
By holy human law, and common troth,
By heaven and earth, and all the power of both,
  That to his borrow'd bed he make retire,
  And stoop to honour, not to foul desire.

Quoth she, " Reward not hospitality
With such black payment as thou hast pretended ;
Mud not the fountain that gave drink to thee ;
Mar not the thing that cannot be amended ;
End thy ill aim, before thy shoot be ended :
  He is no woodman that doth bend his bow
  To strike a poor unseasonable doe.

" My husband is thy friend, for his sake spare me ;
Thyself art mighty, for thine own sake leave me ;
Myself a weakling, do not then ensnare me ;
Thou look'st not like deceit ; do not deceive me :
My sighs, like whirlwinds, labour hence to heave thee.
　　If ever man were mov'd with woman's moans,
　　Be moved with my tears, my sighs, my groans :

" All which together, like a troubled ocean,
Beat at thy rocky and wreck-threatening heart ;
To soften it with their continual motion ;
For stones dissolv'd to water do convert.
O, if no harder than a stone thou art,
　　Melt at my tears, and be compassionate !
　　Soft pity enters at an iron gate.

" In Tarquin's likeness I did entertain thee ;
Hast thou put on his shape to do him shame ?
To all the host of heaven I complain me,
Thou wrong'st his honour, wound'st his princely name
Thou art not what thou seem'st ; and if the same
　　Thou seem'st not what thou art, a god, a king ;
　　For kings like gods should govern everything.

" How will thy shame be seeded in thine age,
When thus thy vices bud before thy spring !
If in thy hope thou dar'st do such outrage,
What dar'st thou not when once thou art a king !
O be remember'd, no outrageous thing
　　From vassal actors can be wip'd away ;
　　Then kings' misdeeds cannot be hid in clay.

42

She bears the load of lust he left behind,
And he the burthen of a guilty mind

" This deed will make thee only lov'd for fear,
But happy monarchs still are fear'd for love :
With foul offenders thou perforce must bear,
When they in thee the like offences prove :
If but for fear of this thy will remove ;
    For princes are the glass, the school, the book,
    Where subjects' eyes do learn, do read, do look.

" And wilt thou be the school where Lust shall learn ?
Must he in thee read lectures of such shame ?
Wilt thou be glass, wherein it shall discern
Authority for sin, warrant for blame,
To privilege dishonour in thy name ?
    Thou back'st reproach against long-lived laud,
    And mak'st fair reputation but a bawd.

" Hast thou command ? by him that gave it thee
From a pure heart command thy rebel will :
Draw not thy sword to guard iniquity,
For it was lent thee all that brood to kill.
Thy princely office how canst thou fulfil,
    When, pattern'd by thy fault, foul Sin may say,
    He learn'd to sin, and thou didst teach the way ?

" Think but how vile a spectacle it were
To view thy present trespass in another.
Men's faults do seldom to themselves appear ;
Their own transgressions partially they smother :
This guilt would seem death-worthy in thy brother.
    O how are they wrapp'd in with infamies,
    That from their own misdeeds askaunce their eyes !

"To thee, to thee, my heav'd-up hands appeal,
Not to seducing lust, thy rash relier ;
I sue for exil'd majesty's repeal ;
Let him return, and flattering thoughts retire :
His true respect will 'prison false desire,
    And wipe the dim mist from thy doting eyne,
    That thou shalt see thy state, and pity mine."

"Have done," quoth he ; "my uncontrolled tide
Turns not, but swells the higher by this let.
Small lights are soon blown out, huge fires abide,
And with the wind in greater fury fret :
The petty streams that pay a daily debt
    To their salt sovereign, with their fresh falls' haste,
    Add to his flow, but alter not his taste."

"Thou art," quoth she, " a sea, a sovereign king ;
And lo, there falls into thy boundless flood
Black lust, dishonour, shame, misgoverning,
Who seek to stain the ocean of thy blood.
If all these petty ills shall change thy good,
    Thy sea within a puddle's womb is hers'd,
    And not the puddle in thy sea dispers'd.

"So shall these slaves be king, and thou their slave ;
Thou nobly base, they basely dignified ;
Thou their fair life, and they thy fouler grave ;
Thou loathed in their shame, they in thy pride :
The lesser thing should not the greater hide ;
    The cedar stoops not to the base shrub's foot,
    But low shrubs wither at the cedar's root.

He faintly flies, sweating with guilty fear;
She stays exclaiming on the direful night

" So let thy thoughts, low vassals to thy state "—
" No more," quoth he, " by heaven, I will not hear thee :
Yield to my love ; if not, enforced hate,
Instead of love's coy touch, shall rudely tear thee ;
That done, despitefully I mean to bear thee
 Unto the base bed of some rascal groom,
 To be thy partner in this shameful doom."

This said, he sets his foot upon the light,
For light and lust are deadly enemies :
Shame folded up in blind concealing night,
When most unseen, then most doth tyrannize.
The wolf hath seiz'd his prey, the poor lamb cries
 Till with her own white fleece her voice controll'd
 Entombs her outcry in her lips' sweet fold :

For with the nightly linen that she wears
He pens her piteous clamours in her head ;
Cooling his hot face in the chastest tears
That ever modest eyes with sorrow shed.
O, that prone lust should stain so pure a bed !
 The spots whereof could weeping purify,
 Her tears should drop on them perpetually.

But she hath lost a dearer thing than life,
And he hath won what he would lose again.
This forced league doth force a further strife,
This momentary joy breeds months of pain,
This hot desire converts to cold disdain :
 Pure Chastity is rifled of her store,
 And Lust, the thief, far poorer than before.

Look, as the full-fed hound or gorged hawk,
Unapt for tender smell or speedy flight,
Make slow pursuit, or altogether balk
The prey wherein by nature they delight ;
So surfeit-taking Tarquin fares this night :
    His taste delicious, in digestion souring,
    Devours his will that liv'd by foul devouring.

O deeper sin than bottomless conceit
Can comprehend in still imagination !
Drunken desire must vomit his receipt,
Ere he can see his own abomination.
While lust is in his pride no exclamation
    Can curb his heat, or rein his rash desire,
    Till, like a jade, self-will himself doth tire.

And then with lank and lean discolour'd cheek,
With heavy eye, knit brow, and strengthless pace,
Feeble desire, all recreant, poor, and meek,
Like to a bankrupt beggar wails his case :
The flesh being proud, desire doth fight with grace,
    For there it revels ; and when that decays,
    The guilty rebel for remission prays.

So fares it with this faultful lord of Rome,
Who this accomplishment so hotly chas'd ;
For now against himself he sounds this doom,
That through the length of times he stands disgrac'd :
Besides, his soul's fair temple is defac'd ;
    To whose weak ruins muster troops of cares,
    To ask the spotted princess how she fares.

50

She says, her subjects with foul insurrection
Have batter'd down her consecrated wall,
And by their mortal fault brought in subjection
Her immortality, and make her thrall
To living death, and pain perpetual :
  Which in her prescience she controlled still,
  But her foresight could not forestall their will.

Even in this thought through the dark night he stealeth,
A captive victor that hath lost in gain ;
Bearing away the wound that nothing healeth,
The scar that will, despite of cure, remain,
Leaving his spoil perplex'd in greater pain.
  She bears the load of lust he left behind,
  And he the burthen of a guilty mind.

He like a thievish dog creeps sadly thence ;
She like a wearied lamb lies panting there ;
He scowls, and hates himself for his offence ;
She, desperate, with her nails her flesh doth tear ;
He faintly flies, sweating with guilty fear ;
  She stays exclaiming on the direful night ;
  He runs, and chides his vanish'd, loath'd delight.

He thence departs a heavy convertite ;
She there remains a hopeless castaway :
He in his speed looks for the morning light ;
She prays she never may behold the day ;
" For day," quoth she, " night's scapes doth open lay ;
  And my true eyes have never practis'd how
  To cloak offences with a cunning brow.

" They think not but that every eye can see
The same disgrace which they themselves behold ;
And therefore would they still in darkness be,
To have their unseen sin remain untold ;
For they their guilt with weeping will unfold,
    And grave, like water, that doth eat in steel,
    Upon my cheeks what helpless shame I feel."

Here she exclaims against repose and rest,
And bids her eyes hereafter still be blind.
She wakes her heart by beating on her breast,
And bids it leap from thence, where it may find
Some purer chest, to close so pure a mind.
    Frantic with grief thus breathes she forth her spite
    Against the unseen secrecy of night :

" O comfort-killing night, image of hell !
Dim register and notary of shame !
Black stage for tragedies and murders fell !
Vast sin-concealing chaos ! nurse of blame !
Blind muffled bawd ! dark harbour for defame !
    Grim cave of death, whispering conspirator,
    With close-tongued treason and the ravisher !

" O hateful, vaporous, and foggy night,
Since thou art guilty of my cureless crime,
Muster thy mists to meet the eastern light,
Make war against proportion'd course of time !
Or if thou wilt permit the sun to climb
    His wonted height, yet ere he go to bed,
    Knit poisonous clouds about his golden head.

52

'The light will show, charácter'd in my brow,
The story of sweet chastity's decay'

" With rotten damps ravish the morning air ;
Let their exhal'd unwholesome breaths make sick
The life of purity, the supreme fair,
Ere he arrive his weary noontide prick ;
And let thy misty vapours march so thick,
  That in their smoky ranks his smother'd light
  May set at noon, and make perpetual night.

" Were Tarquin night, (as he is but night's child,)
The silver-shining queen he would distain ;
Her twinkling handmaids too, by him defil'd,
Through night's black bosom should not peep again ;
So should I have copartners in my pain :
  And fellowship in woe doth woe assuage,
  As palmers' chat makes short their pilgrimage.

" Where now I have no one to blush with me,
To cross their arms, and hang their heads with mine,
To mask their brows, and hide their infamy ;
But I alone alone must sit and pine,
Seasoning the earth with showers of silver brine,
  Mingling my talk with tears, my grief with groans,
  Poor wasting monuments of lasting moans.

" O night, thou furnace of foul-reeking smoke,
Let not the jealous day behold that face
Which underneath thy black all-hiding cloak
Immodestly lies martyr'd with disgrace !
Keep still possession of thy gloomy place,
  That all the faults which in thy reign are made
  May likewise be sepúlchred in thy shade !

55

" Make me not object to the tell-tale day !
The light will show, charácter'd in my brow,
The story of sweet chastity's decay,
The impious breach of holy wedlock vow :
Yea, the illiterate, that know not how
    To 'cipher what is writ in learned books,
    Will quote my loathsome trespass in my looks.

" The nurse, to still her child, will tell my story,
And fright her crying babe with Tarquin's name ;
The orator, to deck his oratory,
Will couple my reproach to Tarquin's shame :
Feast-finding minstrels, tuning my defame,
    Will tie the hearers to attend each line,
    How Tarquin wronged me, I Collatine.

" Let my good name, that senseless reputation,
For Collatine's dear love be kept unspotted :
If that be made a theme for disputation,
The branches of another root are rotted,
And undeserv'd reproach to him allotted,
    That is as clear from this attaint of mine,
    As I, ere this, was pure to Collatine.

" O unseen shame ! invisible disgrace !
O unfelt sore ! crest-wounding, private scar !
Reproach is stamp'd in Collatinus' face,
And Tarquin's eye may read the mot afar,
How he in peace is wounded, not in war.
    Alas, how many bear such shameful blows,
    Which not themselves but he that gives them knows !

56

'Unwholesome weeds take root with precious flowers;
The adder hisses where the sweet birds sing'

" If, Collatine, thine honour lay in me,
From me by strong assault it is bereft.
My honey lost, and I, a drone-like bee,
Have no perfection of my summer left,
But robb'd and ransack'd by injurious theft :
   In thy weak hive a wandering wasp hath crept,
   And suck'd the honey which thy chaste bee kept.

" Yet am I guilty of thy honour's wrack,—
Yet for thy honour did I entertain him ;
Coming from thee, I could not put him back,
For it had been dishonour to disdain him :
Besides of weariness he did complain him,
   And talk'd of virtue :— O, unlook'd for evil,
   When virtue is profan'd in such a devil !

" Why should the worm intrude the maiden bud ?
Or hateful cuckoos hatch in sparrows' nests ?
Or toads infect fair founts with venom mud ?
Or tyrant folly lurk in gentle breasts ?
Or kings be breakers of their own behests ?
   But no perfection is so absolute,
   That some impurity doth not pollute.

" The aged man that coffers up his gold
Is plagued with cramps, and gouts, and painful fits,
And scarce hath eyes his treasure to behold,
But like still-pining Tantalus he sits,
And useless barns the harvest of his wits ;
   Having no other pleasure of his gain
   But torment that it cannot cure his pain.

" So then he hath it, when he cannot use it,
And leaves it to be master'd by his young,
Who in their pride do presently abuse it :
Their father was too weak, and they too strong,
To hold their cursed-blessed fortune long.
　　The sweets we wish for turn to loathed sours,
　　Even in the moment that we call them ours.

" Unruly blasts wait on the tender spring ;
Unwholesome weeds take root with precious flowers ;
The adder hisses where the sweet birds sing ;
What virtue breeds iniquity devours :
We have no good that we can say is ours.
　　But ill-annexed Opportunity
　　Or kills his life, or else his quality.

" O Opportunity ! thy guilt is great :
'T is thou that execut'st the traitor's treason ;
Thou sett'st the wolf where he the lamb may get ;
Whoever plots the sin, thou 'point'st the season ;
'T is thou that spurn'st at right, at law, at reason ;
　　And in thy shady cell, where none may spy him,
　　Sits Sin, to seize the souls that wander by him.

" Thou mak'st the vestal violate her oath ;
Thou blow'st the fire when temperance is thaw'd ;
Thou smother'st honesty, thou murther'st troth ;
Thou foul abetter ! thou notorious bawd !
Thou plantest scandal, and displacest laud :
　　Thou ravisher, thou traitor, thou false thief,
　　Thy honey turns to gall, thy joy to grief !

" Thy secret pleasure turns to open shame,
Thy private feasting to a public fast ;
Thy smoothing titles to a ragged name ;
Thy sugar'd tongue to bitter wormwood taste :
Thy violent vanities can never last.
    How comes it then, vile Opportunity,
    Being so bad, such numbers seek for thee ?

" When wilt thou be the humble suppliant's friend,
And bring him where his suit may be obtain'd ?
When wilt thou sort an hour great strifes to end ?
Or free that soul which wretchedness hath chain'd ?
Give physic to the sick, ease to the pain'd ?
    The poor, lame, blind, halt, creep, cry out for thee ;
    But they ne'er meet with Opportunity.

" The patient dies while the physician sleeps ;
The orphan pines while the oppressor feeds ;
Justice is feasting while the widow weeps ;
Advice is sporting while infection breeds ;
Thou grant'st no time for charitable deeds :
    Wrath, envy, treason, rape, and murder's rages,
    Thy heinous hours wait on them as their pages.

" When truth and virtue have to do with thee
A thousand crosses keep them from thy aid ;
They buy thy help : but Sin ne'er gives a fee,
He gratis comes ; and thou art well appay'd
As well to hear as grant what he hath said.
    My Collatine would else have come to me
    When Tarquin did, but he was stay'd by thee.

" Guilty thou art of murder and of theft ;
Guilty of perjury and subornation ;
Guilty of treason, forgery, and shift ;
Guilty of incest, that abomination :
An accessary by thine inclination
  To all sins past, and all that are to come,
  From the creation to the general doom.

" Mis-shapen Time, copesmate of ugly night,
Swift subtle post, carrier of grisly care,
Eater of youth, false slave to false delight,
Base watch of woes, sin's packhorse, virtue's snare ;
Thou nursest all, and murtherest all that are.
  O hear me then, injurious, shifting Time !
  Be guilty of my death, since of my crime.

" Why hath thy servant, Opportunity,
Betray'd the hours thou gav'st me to repose ?
Cancell'd my fortunes, and enchained me
To endless date of never-ending woes ?
Time's office is to fine the hate of foes ;
  To eat up errors by opinion bred,
  Not spend the dowry of a lawful bed.

" Time's glory is to calm contending kings,
To unmask falsehood, and bring truth to light,
To stamp the seal of time in aged things,
To wake the morn, and sentinel the night,
To wrong the wronger till he render right ;
  To ruinate proud buildings with thy hours,
  And smear with dust their glittering golden towers :

'To make him curse this cursed crimeful night:
Let ghastly shadows his lewd eyes affright'

" To fill with worm-holes stately monuments,
To feed oblivion with decay of things,
To blot old books, and alter their contents,
To pluck the quills from ancient ravens' wings,
To dry the old oak's sap, and cherish springs ;
  To spoil antiquities of hammer'd steel,
  And turn the giddy round of Fortune's wheel ;

" To show the beldame daughters of her daughter,
To make the child a man, the man a child,
To slay the tiger that doth live by slaughter,
To tame the unicorn and lion wild,
To mock the subtle, in themselves beguil'd ;
  To cheer the ploughman with increaseful crops,
  And waste huge stones with little water-drops.

" Why work'st thou mischief in thy pilgrimage,
Unless thou couldst return to make amends ?
One poor retiring minute in an age
Would purchase thee a thousand thousand friends,
Lending him wit that to bad debtors lends :
  O, this dread night, wouldst thou one hour come back,
  I could prevent this storm, and shun thy wrack !

" Thou ceaseless lackey to eternity,
With some mischance cross Tarquin in his flight :
Devise extremes beyond extremity,
To make him curse this cursed crimeful night :
Let ghastly shadows his lewd eyes affright ;
  And the dire thought of his committed evil
  Shape every bush a hideous shapeless devil.

" Disturb his hours of rest with restless trances,
Afflict him in his bed with bedrid groans ;
Let there bechance him pitiful mischances,
To make him moan, but pity not his moans :
Stone him with harden'd hearts, harder than stones ;
    And let mild women to him lose their mildness,
    Wilder to him than tigers in their wildness.

" Let him have time to tear his curled hair,
Let him have time against himself to rave,
Let him have time of Time's help to despair,
Let him have time to live a loathed slave,
Let him have time a beggar's orts to crave ;
    And time to see one that by alms doth live
    Disdain to him disdained scraps to give.

" Let him have time to see. his friends his foes,
And merry fools to mock at him resort ;
Let him have time to mark how slow time goes
In time of sorrow, and how swift and short
His time of folly and his time of sport :
    And ever let his unrecalling crime
    Have time to wail the abusing of his time.

" O Time, thou tutor both to good and bad,
Teach me to curse him that thou taught'st this ill !
At his own shadow let the thief run mad !
Himself himself seek every hour to kill !
Such wretched hands such wretched blood should spill :
    For who so base would such an office have
    As slanderous death's-man to so base a slave ?

'Nor shall he smile at thee in secret thought,
Nor laugh with his companions at thy state'

"The baser is he, coming from a king,
To shame his hope with deeds degenerate.
The mightier man, the mightier is the thing
That makes him honour'd, or begets him hate ;
For greatest scandal waits on greatest state.
　The moon being clouded presently is miss'd,
　But little stars may hide them when they list.

"The crow may bathe his coal-black wings in mire,
And unperceiv'd fly with the filth away ;
But if the like the snow-white swan desire,
The stain upon his silver down will stay.
Poor grooms are sightless night, kings glorious day.
　Gnats are unnoted wheresoe'er they fly,
　But eagles gaz'd upon with every eye.

"Out, idle words, servants to shallow fools !
Unprofitable sounds, weak arbitrators !
Busy yourselves in skill-contending schools,
Debate where leisure serves with dull debaters ;
To trembling clients be you mediators :
　For me, I force not argument a straw,
　Since that my case is past the help of law.

"In vain I rail at Opportunity,
At Time, at Tarquin, and uncheerful night ;
In vain I cavil with my infamy,
In vain I spurn at my confirm'd despite :
This helpless smoke of words doth me no right.
　The remedy indeed to do me good,
　Is to let forth my foul, defiled blood.

69

"Poor hand, why quiver'st thou at this decree?
Honour thyself to rid me of this shame;
For if I die my honour lives in thee,
But if I live thou liv'st in my defame:
Since thou couldst not defend thy loyal dame,
   And wast afear'd to scratch her wicked foe,
   Kill both thyself and her for yielding so."

This said, from her betumbled couch she starteth,
To find some desperate instrument of death:
But this no-slaughter-house no tool imparteth,
To make more vent for passage of her breath,
Which thronging through her lips so vanisheth
   As smoke from Ætna, that in air consumes,
   Or that which from discharged cannon fumes.

"In vain," quoth she, "I live, and seek in vain
Some happy mean to end a hapless life.
I fear'd by Tarquin's falchion to be slain,
Yet for the selfsame purpose seek a knife:
But when I fear'd I was a loyal wife;
   So am I now:—O no, that cannot be;
   Of that true type hath Tarquin rifled me.

"O! that is gone for which I sought to live,
And therefore now I need not fear to die.
To clear this spot by death, at least I give
A badge of fame to slander's livery;
A dying life to living infamy;
   Poor helpless help, the treasure stolen away,
   To burn the guiltless casket where it lay!

"Well, well, dear Collatine, thou shalt not know
The stained taste of violated troth ;
I will not wrong thy true affection so
To flatter thee with an infringed oath ;
This bastard graff shall never come to growth :
    He shall not boast who did thy stock pollute
    That thou art doting father of his fruit.

"Nor shall he smile at thee in secret thought,
Nor laugh with his companions at thy state ;
But thou shalt know thy interest was not bought
Basely with gold, but stolen from forth thy gate.
For me, I am the mistress of my fate,
    And with my trespass never will dispense,
    Till life to death acquit my forc'd offence.

"I will not poison thee with my attaint,
Nor fold my fault in cleanly-coin'd excuses ;
My sable ground of sin I will not paint,
To hide the truth of this false night's abuses :
My tongue shall utter all ; mine eyes like sluices,
    As from a mountain-spring that feeds a dale,
    Shall gush pure streams to purge my impure tale."

By this, lamenting Philomel had ended
The well-tun'd warble of her nightly sorrow,
And solemn night with slow-sad gait descended
To ugly hell ; when lo, the blushing morrow
Lends light to all fair eyes that light will borrow :
    But cloudy Lucrece shames herself to see,
    And therefore still in night would cloister'd be.

Revealing day through every cranny spies,
And seems to point her out where she sits weeping ;
To whom she sobbing speaks : " O eye of eyes,
Why priest thou through my window ? leave thy peeping ;
Mock with thy tickling beams eyes that are sleeping :
　Brand not my forehead with thy piercing light,
　For day hath nought to do what's done by night."

Thus cavils she with everything she sees :
True grief is fond and testy as a child,
Who wayward once, his mood with nought agrees.
Old woes, not infant sorrows, bear them mild ;
Continuance tames the one ; the other wild,
　Like an unpractis'd swimmer plunging still
　With too much labour drowns for want of skill.

So she, deep-drenched in a sea of care,
Holds disputation with each thing she views,
And to herself all sorrow doth compare ;
No object but her passion's strength renews ;
And as one shifts, another straight ensues :
　Sometime her grief is dumb, and hath no words ;
　Sometime 't is mad, and too much talk affords.

The little birds that tune their morning's joy
Make her moans mad with their sweet melody.
For mirth doth search the bottom of annoy ;
Sad souls are slain in merry company ;
Grief best is pleas'd with grief's society :
　True sorrow then is feelingly suffic'd
　When with like semblance it is sympathiz'd.

'*To imitate thee well, against my heart*
Will fix a sharp knife, to affright mine eye'

'T is double death to drown in ken of shore ;
He ten times pines that pines beholding food ;
To see the salve doth make the wound ache more ;
Great grief grieves most at that would do it good ;
Deep woes roll forward like a gentle flood,
    Who, being stopp'd, the bounding banks o'erflows :
    Grief dallied with nor law nor limit knows.

" You mocking birds," quoth she, " your tunes entomb
Within your hollow-swelling feather'd breasts,
And in my hearing be you mute and dumb !
(My restless discord loves no stops nor rests ;
A woeful hostess brooks not merry guests :)
    Relish your nimble notes to pleasing ears ;
    Distress likes dumps when time is kept with tears.

" Come, Philomel, that sing'st of ravishment,
Make thy sad grove in my dishevell'd hair.
As the dank earth weeps at thy languishment,
So I at each sad strain will strain a tear,
And with deep groans the diapason bear :
    For burthen-wise I'll hum on Tarquin still,
    While thou on Tereus descant'st better skill.

" And whiles against a thorn thou bear'st thy part,
To keep thy sharp woes waking, wretched I,
To imitate thee well, against my heart
Will fix a sharp knife, to affright mine eye ;
Who, if it wink, shall thereon fall and die.
    These means, as frets upon an instrument,
    Shall tune our heartstrings to true languishment.

75

" And for, poor bird, thou sing'st not in the day,
As shaming any eye should thee behold,
Some dark deep desert, seated from the way,
That knows nor parching heat nor freezing cold,
We will find out ; and there we will unfold
    To creatures stern sad tunes, to change their kinds :
    Since men prove beasts let beasts bear gentle minds."

As the poor frighted deer, that stands at gaze,
Wildly determining which way to fly,
Or one encompass'd with a winding maze,
That cannot tread the way out readily ;
So with herself is she in mutiny,
    To live or die which of the twain were better,
    When life is sham'd, and Death reproach's debtor.

" To kill myself," quoth she, " alack ! what were it,
But with my body my poor soul's pollution ?
They that lose half with greater patience bear it
Than they whose whole is swallow'd in confusion.
That mother tries a merciless conclusion
    Who, having two sweet babes, when death takes one,
    Will slay the other, and be nurse to none.

" My body or my soul, which was the dearer ?
When the one pure, the other made divine.
Whose love of either to myself was nearer ?
When both were kept for heaven and Collatine.
Ah me ! the bark peel'd from the lofty pine,
    His leaves will wither, and his sap decay ;
    So must my soul, her bark being peel'd away.

But as the earth doth weep, the sun being set,
Each flower moisten'd like a melting eye

" Her house is sack'd, her quiet interrupted,
Her mansion batter'd by the enemy ;
Her sacred temple spotted, spoil'd, corrupted,
Grossly engirt with daring infamy :
Then let it not be call'd impiety.
    If in this blemish'd fort I make some hole
    Through which I may convey this troubled soul.

" Yet die I will not till my Collatine
Have heard the cause of my untimely death ;
That he may vow, in that sad hour of mine,
Revenge on him that made me stop my breath.
My stained blood to Tarquin I'll bequeath,
    Which by him tainted shall for him be spent,
    And as his due writ in my testament.

" My honour I'll bequeath unto the knife
That wounds my body so dishonoured.
'T is honour to deprive dishonour'd life ;
The one will live, the other being dead :
So of shame's ashes shall my fame be bred ;
    For in my death I murther shameful scorn :
    My shame so dead, mine honour is new-born.

" Dear lord of that dear jewel I have lost,
What legacy shall I bequeath to thee ?
My resolution, Love, shall be thy boast,
By whose example thou reveng'd mayst be.
How Tarquin must be used, read it in me :
    Myself, thy friend, will kill myself, thy foe,
    And, for my sake, serve thou false Tarquin so.

" This brief abridgment of my will I make :
My soul and body to the skies and ground ;
My resolution, husband, do thou take ;
Mine honour be the knife's that makes my wound ;
My shame be his that did my fame confound ;
  And all my fame that lives disbursed be
  To those that live, and think no shame of me.

" Thou, Collatine, shalt oversee this will ;
How was I overseen that thou shalt see it !
My blood shall wash the slander of mine ill ;
My life's foul deed my life's fair end shall free it.
Faint not faint heart, but stoutly say, ' so be it.'
  Yield to my hand ; my hand shall conquer thee ;
  Thou dead, both die, and both shall victors be."

This plot of death when sadly she had laid,
And wip'd the brinish pearl from her bright eyes,
With untun'd tongue she hoarsely call'd her maid,
Whose swift obedience to her mistress hies ;
For fleet-wing'd duty with thought's feathers flies.
  Poor Lucrece' cheeks unto her maid seem so
  As winter meads when sun doth melt their snow.

Her mistress she doth give demure good-morrow,
With soft-slow tongue, true mark of modesty,
And sorts a sad look to her lady's sorrow,
(For why ? her face wore sorrow's livery,)
But durst not ask of her audaciously
  Why her two suns were cloud-eclipsed so,
  Nor why her fair cheeks over-wash'd with woe.

But as the earth doth weep, the sun being set,
Each flower moisten'd like a melting eye ;
Even so the maid with swelling drops 'gan wet
Her circled eyne, enforc'd by sympathy
Of those fair suns, set in her mistress' sky,
  Who in a salt-wav'd ocean quench their light,
  Which makes the maid weep like the dewy night.

A pretty while these pretty creatures stand,
Like ivory conduits coral cisterns filling :
One justly weeps ; the other takes in hand
No cause, but company, of her drops spilling :
Their gentle sex to weep are often willing ;
  Grieving themselves to guess at others' smarts,
  And then they drown their eyes, or break their hearts.

For men have marble, women waxen minds,
And therefore are they form'd as marble will ;
The weak oppress'd, the impression of strange kinds
Is form'd in them by force, by fraud, or skill :
Then call them not the authors of their ill,
  No more than wax shall be accounted evil,
  Wherein is stamp'd the semblance of a devil.

Their smoothness, like a goodly champaign plain,
Lays open all the little worms that creep ;
In men, as in a rough-grown grove, remain
Cave-keeping evils that obscurely sleep :
Through crystal walls each little mote will peep :
  Though men can cover crimes with bold stern looks,
  Poor women's faces are their own faults' books.

No man inveigh against the wither'd flower,
But chide rough winter that the flower hath kill'd !
Not that devour'd, but that which doth devour
Is worthy blame. O, let it not be hild
Poor women's faults that they are so fulfill'd
   With men's abuses ! those proud lords, to blame,
   Make weak-made women tenants to their shame.

The precedent whereof in Lucrece view,
Assail'd by night with circumstances strong
Of present death, and shame that might ensue
By that her death, to do her husband wrong :
Such danger to resistance did belong,
   That dying fear through all her body spread ;
   And who cannot abuse a body dead ?

By this, mild patience bid fair Lucrece speak
To the poor counterfeit of her complaining :
" My girl," quoth she, " on what occasion break
Those tears from thee, that down thy cheeks are raining ?
If thou dost weep for grief of my sustaining,
   Know, gentle wench, it small avails my mood :
   If tears could help mine own would do me good.

" But tell me, girl, when went "—(and there she stay'd
Till after a deep groan) " Tarquin from hence ? "
" Madam, ere I was up," replied the maid,
" The more to blame my sluggard negligence :
Yet with the fault I thus far can dispense ;
   Myself was stirring ere the break of day,
   And, ere I rose, was Tarquin gone away.

Her maid is gone, and she prepares to write,
First hovering o'er the paper with her quill

" But, lady, if your maid may be so bold,
She would request to know your heaviness."
" O peace ! " quoth Lucrece ; " if it should be told,
The repetition cannot make it less ;
For more it is than I can well express :
  And that deep torture may be call'd a hell,
  When more is felt than one hath power to tell.

" Go, get me hither paper, ink, and pen—
Yet save that labour, for I have them here.
What should I say ?—One of my husband's men
Bid thou be ready, by and by, to bear
A letter to my lord, my love, my dear ;
  Bid him with speed prepare to carry it :
  The cause craves haste, and it will soon be writ."

Her maid is gone, and she prepares to write,
First hovering o'er the paper with her quill :
Conceit and grief an eager combat fight ;
What wit sets down is blotted straight with will ;
This is too curious-good, this blunt and ill :
  Much like a press of people at a door,
  Throng her inventions, which shall be before.

At last she thus begins :—" Thou worthy lord
Of that unworthy wife that greeteth thee,
Health to thy person ! next vouchsafe to afford
(If ever, love, thy Lucrece thou wilt see)
Some present speed to come and visit me :
  So I commend me from our house in grief ;
  My woes are tedious, though my words are brief."

Here folds she up the tenor of her woe,
Her certain sorrow writ uncertainly.
By this short schedule Collatine may know
Her grief, but not her grief's true quality;
She dares not thereof make discovery,
　　Lest he should hold it her own gross abuse,
　　Ere she with blood had stain'd her stain'd excuse.

Besides, the life and feeling of her passion
She hoards, to spend when he is by to hear her;
When sighs, and groans, and tears may grace the fashion
Of her disgrace, the better so to clear her
From that suspicion which the world might bear her.
　　To shun this blot, she would not blot the letter
　　With words, till action might become them better.

To see sad sights moves more than hear them told;
For then the eye interprets to the ear
The heavy motion that it doth behold,
When every part a part of woe doth bear.
'T is but a part of sorrow that we hear:
　　Deep sounds make lesser noise than shallow fords,
　　And sorrow ebbs, being blown with wind of words.

Her letter now is seal'd, and on it writ,
" At Ardea to my lord with more than haste : "
The post attends, and she delivers it,
Charging the sour-fac'd groom to hie as fast
As lagging fowls before the northern blast.
　　Speed more than speed but dull and slow she deems:
　　Extremity still urgeth such extremes.

THOU · WORTHY · LORD · OF · THAT · UNW
ORTHY · WIFE · T[...] · GREETETH · THEE ·
HEALTH · [...] · [...]
THO[...]
WI[...]
B[...]

Charging the sour-fac'd groom to hie as fast
As lagging fowls before the northern blast

The homely villein court'sies to her low ;
And blushing on her, with a steadfast eye
Receives the scroll, without or yea or no,
And forth with bashful innocence doth hie.
But they whose guilt within their bosoms lie
  Imagine every eye beholds their blame ;
  For Lucrece thought he blush'd to see her shame ;

When, silly groom ! God wot, it was defect
Of spirit, life, and bold audacity.
Such harmless creatures have a true respect
To talk in deeds, while others saucily
Promise more speed, but do it leisurely :
  Even so, this pattern of the worn-out age
  Pawn'd honest looks, but laid no words to gage.

His kindled duty kindled her mistrust,
That two red fires in both their faces blaz'd ;
She thought he blush'd, as knowing Tarquin's lust,
And, blushing with him, wistly on him gaz'd ;
Her earnest eye did make him more amaz'd :
  The more she saw the blood his cheeks replenish,
  The more she thought he spied in her some blemish.

But long she thinks till he return again,
And yet the duteous vassal scarce is gone.
The weary time she cannot entertain,
For now 't is stale to sigh, to weep, and groan :
So woe hath wearied woe, moan tired moan,
  That she her plaints a little while doth stay,
  Pausing for means to mourn some newer way.

At last she calls to mind where hangs a piece
Of skilful painting, made for Priam's Troy ;
Before the which is drawn the power of Greece,
For Helen's rape the city to destroy,
Threat'ning cloud-kissing Ilion with annoy ;
    Which the conceited painter drew so proud,
    As heaven (it seem'd) to kiss the turrets bow'd.

A thousand lamentable objects there,
In scorn of Nature, Art gave lifeless life :
Many a dry drop seem'd a weeping tear,
Shed for the slaughter'd husband by the wife :
The red blood reek'd to show the painter's strife ;
    And dying eyes gleam'd forth their ashy lights,
    Like dying coals burnt out in tedious nights.

There might you see the labouring pioneer
Begrim'd with sweat, and smeared all with dust ;
And from the towers of Troy there would appear
The very eyes of men through loopholes thrust,
Gazing upon the Greeks with little lust :
    Such sweet observance in this work was had,
    That one might see those far-off eyes look sad.

In great commanders grace and majesty
You might behold, triúmphing in their faces ;
In youth, quick bearing and dexterity ;
And here and there the painter interlaces
Pale cowards, marching on with trembling paces ;
    Which heartless peasants did so well resemble,
    That one would swear he saw them quake and tremble.

In Ajax and Ulysses, O what art
Of physiognomy might one behold !
The face of either 'cipher'd either's heart ;
Their face their manners most expressly told :
In Ajax' eyes blunt rage and rigour roll'd ;
    But the mild glance that sly Ulysses lent
    Show'd deep regard and smiling government.

There pleading might you see grave Nestor stand,
As 't were encouraging the Greeks to fight ;
Making such sober action with his hand
That it beguil'd attention, charm'd the sight :
In speech, it seem'd, his beard all silver white
    Wagg'd up and down, and from his lips did fly
    Thin winding breath, which purl'd up to the sky.

About him were a press of gaping faces,
Which seem'd to swallow up his sound advice ;
All jointly listening, but with several graces,
As if some mermaid did their ears entice ;
Some high, some low, the painter was so nice :
    The scalps of many, almost hid behind,
    To jump up higher seem'd to mock the mind.

Here one man's hand lean'd on another's head,
His nose being shadow'd by his neighbour's ear ;
Here one being throng'd bears back, all boll'n and red ;
Another smother'd seems to pelt and swear ;
And in their rage such signs of rage they bear,
    As, but for loss of Nestor's golden words,
    It seem'd they would debate with angry swords.

For much imaginary work was there ;
Conceit deceitful, so compact, so kind,
That for Achilles' image stood his spear,
Grip'd in an armed hand ; himself, behind,
Was left unseen, save to the eye of mind :
    A hand, a foot, a face, a leg, a head,
    Stood for the whole to be imagined.

And from the walls of strong besieged Troy
When their brave hope, bold Hector, march'd to field,
Stood many Trojan mothers, sharing joy
To see their youthful sons bright weapons wield ;
And to their hope they such odd action yield,
    That through their light joy seemed to appear
    (Like bright things stain'd) a kind of heavy fear.

And, from the strond of Dardan where they fought,
To Simois' reedy banks, the red blood ran,
Whose waves to imitate the battle sought
With swelling ridges ; and their ranks began
To break upon the galled shore, and than
    Retire again, till meeting greater ranks
    They join, and shoot their foam at Simois' banks.

To this well-painted piece is Lucrece come,
To find a face where all distress is stel'd.
Many she sees where cares have carved some,
But none where all distress and dolour dwell'd,
Till she despairing Hecuba beheld,
    Staring on Priam's wounds with her old eyes,
    Which bleeding under Pyrrhus' proud foot lies.

Here, all enrag'd, such passion her assails . . .
She tears the senseless Sinon with her nails

In her the painter had anatomiz'd
Time's ruin, beauty's wrack, and grim care's reign;
Her cheeks with chaps and wrinkles were disguis'd;
Of what she was no semblance did remain:
Her blue blood, chang'd to black in every vein,
    Wanting the spring that those shrunk pipes had fed,
    Show'd life imprison'd in a body dead.

On this sad shadow Lucrece spends her eyes,
And shapes her sorrow to the beldame's woes,
Who nothing wants to answer her but cries,
And bitter words to ban her cruel foes:
The painter was no God to lend her those;
    And therefore Lucrece swears he did her wrong,
    To give her so much grief, and not a tongue.

"Poor instrument," quoth she, "without a sound,
I'll tune thy woes with my lamenting tongue:
And drop sweet balm in Priam's painted wound,
And rail on Pyrrhus that hath done him wrong,
And with my tears quench Troy that burns so long;
    And with my knife scratch out the angry eyes
    Of all the Greeks that are thine enemies.

"Show me the strumpet that began this stir,
That with my nails her beauty I may tear.
Thy heat of lust, fond Paris, did incur
This load of wrath that burning Troy doth bear;
Thy eye kindled the fire that burneth here:
    And here in Troy, for trespass of thine eye,
    The sire, the son, the dame, and daughter, die.

" Why should the private pleasure of some one
Become the public plague of many mo?
Let sin, alone committed, light alone
Upon his head that hath transgressed so.
Let guiltless souls be freed from guilty woe :
   For one's offence why should so many fall,
   To plague a private sin in general ?

" Lo, here weeps Hecuba, here Priam dies,
Here manly Hector faints, here Troilus swounds ;
Here friend by friend in bloody channel lies,
And friend to friend gives unadvised wounds,
And one man's lust these many lives confounds :
   Had doting Priam check'd his son's desire,
   Troy had been bright with fame, and not with fire."

Here feelingly she weeps Troy's painted woes :
For sorrow, like a heavy-hanging bell,
Once set on ringing, with his own weight goes ;
Then little strength rings out the doleful knell :
So Lucrece set a-work sad tales doth tell
   To pencill'd pensiveness and colour'd sorrow ;
   She lends them words, and she their looks doth borrow.

She throws her eyes about the painting, round,
And whom she finds forlorn she doth lament :
At last she sees a wretched image bound,
That piteous looks to Phrygian shepherds lent ;
His face, though full of cares, yet show'd content :
   Onward to Troy with the blunt swains he goes,
   So mild that Patience seem'd to scorn his woes.

'*Sweet love, what spite hath thy fair colour spent?*
Why art thou thus attir'd in discontent?'.

In him the painter labour'd with his skill
To hide deceit, and give the harmless show
An humble gait, calm looks, eyes wailing still,
A brow unbent, that seem'd to welcome woe ;
Cheeks neither red nor pale, but mingled so
      That blushing red no guilty instance gave,
      Nor ashy pale the fear that false hearts have.

But, like a constant and confirmed devil,
He entertain'd a show so seeming just,
And therein so ensconc'd his secret evil,
That jealousy itself could not mistrust
False-creeping craft and perjury should thrust
      Into so bright a day such black-fac'd storms,
      Or blot with hell-born sin such saint-like forms.

The well-skill'd workman this mild image drew
For perjur'd Sinon, whose enchanting story
The credulous old Priam after slew ;
Whose words, like wildfire, burnt the shining glory
Of rich-built Ilion, that the skies were sorry,
      And little stars shot from their fixed places,
      When their glass fell wherein they view'd their faces.

This picture she advisedly perus'd,
And chid the painter for his wondrous skill ;
Saying, some shape in Sinon's was abus'd,
So fair a form lodg'd not a mind so ill ;
And still on him she gaz'd, and gazing still,
      Such signs of truth in his plain face she spied,
      That she concludes the picture was belied.

" It cannot be," quoth she, " that so much guile "—
(She would have said) " can lurk in such a look ; "
But Tarquin's shape came in her mind the while,
And from her tongue " can lurk " from " cannot " took ;
" It cannot be " she in that sense forsook,
  And turn'd it thus : " It cannot be, I find,
  But such a face should bear a wicked mind :

" For even as subtle Sinon here is painted,
So sober-sad, so weary, and so mild,
(As if with grief or travail he had fainted,)
To me came Tarquin armed ; so beguil'd
With outward honesty, but yet defil'd
  With inward vice : as Priam him did cherish,
  So did I Tarquin ; so my Troy did perish.

" Look, look, how listening Priam wets his eyes,
To see those borrow'd tears that Sinon sheds.
Priam, why art thou old, and yet not wise ?
For every tear he falls a Trojan bleeds ;
His eye drops fire, no water thence proceeds :
  Those round clear pearls of his that move thy pity
  Are balls of quenchless fire to burn thy city.

" Such devils steal effects from lightless hell ;
For Sinon in his fire doth quake with cold,
And in that cold hot-burning fire doth dwell ;
These contraries such unity do hold
Only to flatter fools, and make them bold :
  So Priam's trust false Sinon's tears doth flatter,
  That he finds means to burn his Troy with water."

Here, all enrag'd, such passion her assails,
That patience is quite beaten from her breast.
She tears the senseless Sinon with her nails,
Comparing him to that unhappy guest
Whose deed hath made herself herself detest :
    As last she smilingly with this gives o'er ;
    " Fool ! fool ! " quoth she, " his wounds will not be sore."

Thus ebbs and flows the current of her sorrow,
And time doth weary time with her complaining.
She looks for night, and then she longs for morrow,
And both she thinks too long with her remaining :
Short time seems long in sorrow's sharp sustaining.
    Though woe be heavy yet it seldom sleeps ;
    And they that watch see time how slow it creeps.

Which all this time hath overslipp'd her thought,
That she with painted images hath spent :
Being from the feeling of her own grief brought
By deep surmise of others' detriment ;
Losing her woes in shows of discontent.
    It easeth some, though none it ever cur'd,
    To think their dolour others have endur'd.

But now the mindful messenger, come back,
Brings home his lord and other company ;
Who finds his Lucrece clad in mourning black ;
And round about her tear-distained eye
Blue circles stream'd, like rainbows in the sky.
    These water-galls in her dim element
    Foretell new storms to those already spent.

Which when her sad-beholding husband saw,
Amazedly in her sad face he stares :
Her eyes, though sod in tears, look'd red and raw,
Her lively colour kill'd with deadly cares.
He hath no power to ask her how she fares, .
   But stood, like old acquaintance in a trance,
   Met far from home, wondering each other's chance.

At last he takes her by the bloodless hand,
And thus begins: " What uncouth ill event
Hath thee befallen, that thou dost trembling stand ?
Sweet love, what spite hath thy fair colour spent ?
Why art thou thus attir'd in discontent ?
   Unmask, dear dear, this moody heaviness,
   And tell thy grief, that we may give redress."

Three times with sighs she gives her sorrow fire
Ere once she can discharge one word of woe :
At length address'd to answer his desire,
She modestly prepares to let them know
Her honour is ta'en prisoner by the foe ;
   While Collatine and his consorted lords
   With sad attention long to hear her words.

And now this pale swan in her watery nest
Begins the sad dirge of her certain ending :
" Few words," quoth she, " shall fit the trespass best,
Where no excuse can give the fault amending :
In me more woes than words are now depending ;
   And my laments would be drawn out too long,
   To tell them all with one poor tired tongue.

She utters this: 'He, he, fair lords, 't is he,
That guides this hand to give this wound to me'

" Then be this all the task it hath to say :—
Dear husband, in the interest of thy bed
A stranger came, and on that pillow lay
Where thou wast wont to rest thy weary head ;
And what wrong else may be imagined
　　By foul enforcement might be done to me,
　　From that, alas ! thy Lucrece is not free.

" For in the dreadful dead of dark midnight,
With shining falchion in my chamber came
A creeping creature, with a flaming light,
And softly cried, ' Awake, thou Roman dame,
And entertain my love ; else lasting shame
　　On thee and thine this night I will inflict,
　　If thou my love's desire do contradict.

" ' For some hard-favour'd groom of thine,' quoth he,
' Unless thou yoke thy liking to my will,
I'll murder straight, and then I'll slaughter thee,
And swear I found you where you did fulfil
The loathsome act of lust, and so did kill
　　The lechers in their deed : this act will be
　　My fame, and thy perpetual infamy.'

" With this I did begin to start and cry,
And then against my heart he set his sword,
Swearing, unless I took all patiently
I should not live to speak another word :
So should my shame still rest upon record,
　　And never be forgot in mighty Rome
　　The adulterate death of Lucrece and her groom.

" Mine enemy was strong, my poor self weak,
And far the weaker with so strong a fear :
My bloody judge forbade my tongue to speak ;
No rightful plea might plead for justice there :
His scarlet lust came evidence to swear
   That my poor beauty had purloin'd his eyes,
   And when the judge is robb'd, the prisoner dies.

" O teach me how to make mine own excuse !
Or, at the least, this refuge let me find ;
Though my gross blood be stain'd with this abuse,
Immaculate and spotless is my mind ;
That was not forc'd ; that never was inclin'd
   To accessary yieldings, but still pure
   Doth in her poison'd closet yet endure."

Lo here, the hopeless merchant of this loss,
With head declin'd, and voice damm'd up with woe,
With sad-set eyes, and wretched arms across,
From lips new-waxen pale begins to blow
The grief away that stops his answer so :
   But wretched as he is he strives in vain ;
   What he breathes out his breath drinks up again.

As through an arch the violent roaring tide
Outruns the eye that doth behold his haste ;
Yet in the eddy boundeth in his pride
Back to the strait that forc'd him on so fast ;
In rage sent out, recall'd in rage, being past :
   Even so he sighs, his sorrows make a saw,
   To push grief on, and back the same grief draw.

Which speechless woe of his poor she attendeth,
And his untimely frenzy thus awaketh :
" Dear lord, thy sorrow to my sorrow lendeth
Another power ; no flood by raining slaketh.
My woe too sensible thy passion maketh
   More feeling-painful : let it then suffice
   To drown one woe, one pair of weeping eyes.

" And for my sake, when I might charm thee so,
For she that was thy Lucrece,—now attend me ;
Be suddenly revenged on my foe,
Thine, mine, his own ; suppose thou dost defend me
From what is past : the help that thou shalt lend me
   Comes all too late, yet let the traitor die ;
   For sparing justice feeds iniquity.

" But ere I name him, you, fair lords," quoth she,
(Speaking to those that came with Collatine)
" Shall plight your honourable faiths to me,
With swift pursuit to venge this wrong of mine ;
For 't is a meritorious fair design
   To chase injustice with revengeful arms :
   Knights, by their oaths, should right poor ladies' harms."

At this request, with noble disposition
Each present lord began to promise aid,
As bound in knighthood to her imposition,
Longing to hear the hateful foe bewray'd.
But she, that yet her sad task hath not said,
   The protestation stops. " O speak," quoth she,
   " How may this forced stain be wip'd from me ?

"What is the quality of mine offence,
Being constrain'd with dreadful circumstance?
May my pure mind with the foul act dispense,
My low-declined honour to advance?
May any terms acquit me from this chance?
  The poison'd fountain clears itself again;
  And why not I from this compelled stain?"

With this, they all at once began to say,
Her body's stain her mind untainted clears;
While with a joyless smile she turns away
The face, that map which deep impression bears
Of hard misfortune, carv'd in it with tears.
  "No, no," quoth she, "no dame, hereafter living,
  By my excuse shall claim excuse's giving."

Here with a sigh, as if her heart would break,
She throws forth Tarquin's name: "He, he," she says,
But more than "he" her poor tongue could not speak;
Till after many accents and delays,
Untimely breathings, sick and short assays,
  She utters this: "He, he, fair lords, 't is he,
  That guides this hand to give this wound to me."

Even here she sheathed in her harmless breast
A harmful knife, that thence her soul unsheath'd:
That blow did bail it from the deep unrest
Of that polluted prison where it breath'd:
Her contrite sighs unto the clouds bequeath'd
  Her winged sprite, and through her wounds doth fly
  Life's lasting date from cancell'd destiny.

'*Now, by the Capitol that we adore . . .*
We will revenge the death of this true wife'

Stone-still, astonish'd with this deadly deed,
Stood Collatine and all his lordly crew ;
Till Lucrece' father, that beholds her bleed,
Himself on her self-slaughter'd body threw ;
And from the purple fountain Brutus drew
   The murderous knife, and as it left the place,
   Her blood, in poor revenge, held it in chase ;

And bubbling from her breast, it doth divide
In two slow rivers, that the crimson blood
Circles her body in on every side,
Who like a late-sack'd island vastly stood
Bare and unpeopled, in this fearful flood.
   Some of her blood still pure and red remain'd,
   And some look'd black, and that false Tarquin stain'd.

About the mourning and congealed face
Of that black blood a watery rigol goes,
Which seems to weep upon the tainted place :
And ever since, as pitying Lucrece' woes,
Corrupted blood some watery token shows ;
   And blood untainted still doth red abide,
   Blushing at that which is so putrefied.

" Daughter, dear daughter," old Lucretius cries,
" That life was mine which thou hast here depriv'd.
If in the child the father's image lies,
Where shall I live now Lucrece is unliv'd ?
Thou was not to this end from me deriv'd.
   If children predecease progenitors,
   We are their offspring, and they none of ours.

" Poor broken glass, I often did behold
In thy sweet semblance my old age new born ;
But now that fair fresh mirror, dim and old,
Shows me a barebon'd death by time outworn ;
O, from thy cheeks my image thou hast torn !
  And shiver'd all the beauty of my glass,
  That I no more can see what once I was.

" O time, cease thou thy course, and last no longer,
If they surcease to be that should survive.
Shall rotten death make conquest of the stronger,
And leave the faltering feeble souls alive ?
The old bees die, the young possess their hive :
  Then live, sweet Lucrece, live again, and see
  Thy father die, and not thy father thee ? "

By this starts Collatine as from a dream,
And bids Lucretius give his sorrow place ;
And then in key-cold Lucrece' bleeding stream
He falls, and bathes the pale fear in his face,
And counterfeits to die with her a space ;
  Till manly shame bids him possess his breath,
  And live, to be revenged on her death.

The deep vexation of his inward soul
Hath serv'd a dumb arrest upon his tongue ;
Who, mad that sorrow should his use control,
Or keep him from heart-easing words so long,
Begins to talk ; but through his lips do throng
  Weak words, so thick come, in his poor heart's aid,
  That no man could distinguish what he said.

Yet sometime Tarquin was pronounced plain,
But through his teeth, as if the name he tore.
This windy tempest, till it blow up rain,
Held back his sorrow's tide, to make it more ;
At last it rains, and busy winds give o'er :
    Then son and father weep with equal strife,
    Who should weep most for daughter or for wife.

The one doth call her his, the other his,
Yet neither may possess the claim they lay.
The father says, " She's mine." " O, mine she is,"
Replies her husband : " do not take away
My sorrow's interest ; let no mourner say
    He weeps for her, for she was only mine,
    And only must be wail'd by Collatine."

" O," quoth Lucretius, " I did give that life
Which she too early and too late hath spill'd."
" Woe, woe," quoth Collatine, " she was my wife,
I ow'd her, and 't is mine that she hath kill'd."
" My daughter " and " my wife " with clamours fill'd
    The dispers'd air, who, holding Lucrece' life,
    Answer'd their cries, " my daughter " and " my wife."

Brutus, who pluck'd the knife from Lucrece' side,
Seeing such emulation in their woe,
Began to clothe his wit in state and pride,
Burying in Lucrece' wound his folly's show.
He with the Romans was esteemed so
    As silly jeering idiots are with kings,
    For sportive words, and uttering foolish things.

But now he throws that shallow habit by,
Wherein deep policy did him disguise ;
And arm'd his long-hid wits advisedly,
To check the tears in Collatinus' eyes.
" Thou wronged lord of Rome," quoth he, " arise ;
    Let my unsounded self, suppos'd a fool,
    Now set thy long-experienc'd wit to school.

" Why, Collatine, is woe the cure for woe ?
Do wounds help wounds, or grief help grievous deeds ?
Is it revenge to give thyself a blow,
For his foul act by whom thy fair wife bleeds ?
Such childish humour from weak minds proceeds :
    Thy wretched wife mistook the matter so,
    To slay herself, that should have slain her foe.

" Courageous Roman, do not steep thy heart
In such relenting dew of lamentations,
But kneel with me, and help to bear thy part,
To rouse our Roman gods with invocations,
That they will suffer these abominations,
    (Since Rome herself in them doth stand disgrac'd,)
    By our strong arms from forth her fair streets chas'd.

" Now, by the Capitol that we adore,
And by this chaste blood so unjustly stain'd,
By heaven's fair sun that breeds the fat earth's store,
By all our country rights in Rome maintain'd,
And by chaste Lucrece' soul that late complain'd
    Her wrongs to us, and by this bloody knife,
    We will revenge the death of this true wife."